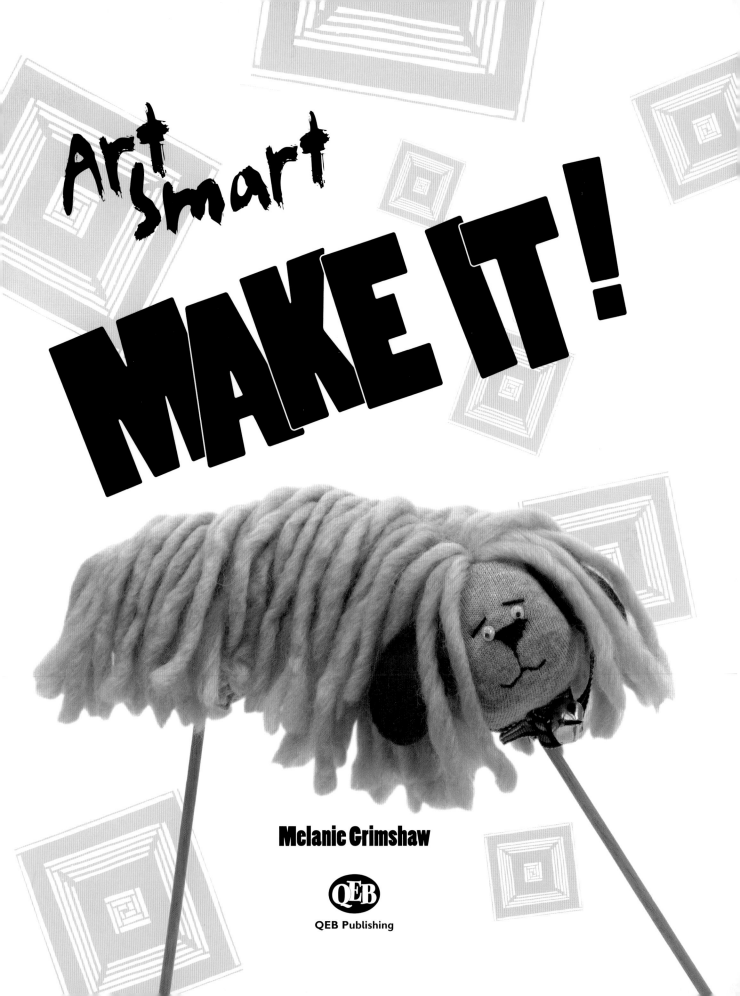

Art Smart

MAKE IT!

Melanie Grimshaw

QEB

QEB Publishing

Editor: Lauren Taylor
Design: Tall Tree Ltd www.talltreebooks.co.uk
Illustrator: Tom Connell

Copyright © QED Publishing 2012

Published in the United States by
QEB Publishing, Inc.
3 Wrigley, Suite A
Irvine, CA 92618

www.qed-publishing.co.uk

A CIP record for this book is available from the
Library of Congress.

ISBN 978 1 60992 274 0

Printed in China

Picture credits

(t=top, b=bottom, l=left, r=right, c=center, fc=front cover, bc=back cover)
Mark Winwood: 5br, 13b, 25br
Philip Wilkins: 7c, 9b, 11l, 15br, 17bl, 19b, 21bl, 23br, 27b,
Shutterstock: fctl, bctl, akiyoko; fctl SeDmi; fctl oksix; fctc, bctr,
oksana2010; fctr Madlen; fcc, bctl, bctc, Iwona Grodzka; fccr, bctr,
Kitch Bain; fctr, 3cl, 4c SeDmi; fcc, bcb, 3tr, 20tr, 20br, 14t, 14c, 31bl,
Jenny Solomon; fcbl, bccl, 3cr, 22tc, 22br, Garsya; fcbl, 3bl, 24br,
Vasily Kovalev; fcbr, 6, 26br, 30tr Picsfive; fccl, bctc, 10cl pukach; 3tl,
3cb, 18cr jcjgphotography; 3br Denis and Yulia Pogostins; 8tr
Picsfive; 10cr, 16tr shutswis; 13tl magicoven; 16br, 26tc, pukach

Note to Adults:
Some children might be able to
do some or all of these projects
on their own, while others might
need more help. These are
projects that you can work on
together, not only to avoid any
problems or accidents, but also
to share in the fun of making art.

At the top of the page for each project you will
find this handy key. It will tell you the difficulty
level to expect from each project:

Quick Creative Fix
These projects are quick, easy and perfect for
a beginner.

Sharpen Your Skills
Confident with your beginner skills? Move onto
these slightly tougher projects.

Ready For a Challenge
For a challenging project you can really get
stuck into.

Creative Masterpiece
Think you can tackle the toughest textile
projects? Have a go at these.

CONTENTS

LOVE-HEART GIFT BOX

Is a special occasion coming up? This cute gift box will be a great way to present your gift!

1 For the heart, cut out two equal-sized pieces of felt. Pin these two pieces together.

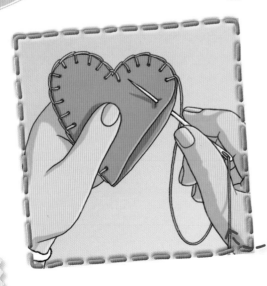

2 Using a needle and thread, stitch the heart pieces together using a blanket stitch. Leave a small space to insert your toy stuffing, then stitch it completely closed when you have stuffed the heart.

3 Wrap a length of ribbon around the outside of your box, and secure it with fabric glue. You should also stitch on one or two separate felt heart shapes to the ribbon.

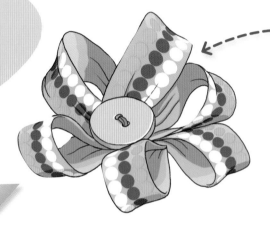

4 Gather a length of ribbon together in loops to create a flower shape. Stitch a button in the center to hold the ribbon in place.

5 Finally, glue the stuffed felt heart and ribbon flower to the box lid using fabric glue.

Make an Easter-themed box using colorful feathers for a cute Easter chick!

5

WOVEN MOBILE

This mobile will add a splash of color to your bedroom, and it's lots of fun to make!

YOU WILL NEED:

- Balls of yarn in assorted colors
- Wooden dowel rods of various lengths
- Scissors
- Colored beads

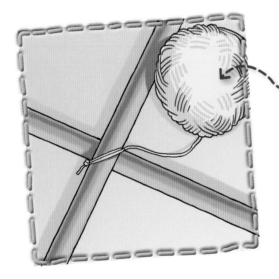

1 With the end of a small ball of yarn, tie a knot around the center of two dowel rods. Secure the rods into a cross shape.

2 Weave the yarn over and around one dowel rod, then over and around the next, and so on with each rod. Make sure to keep the wool taut and keep your rods in the cross position.

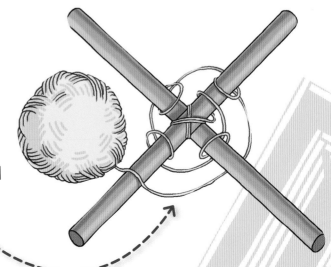

3 Keep weaving and tie on new colors of yarn to make a striped effect. Stop when you have an inch or two of space left at both ends of each rod. Tie the loose end of the yarn in a knot to secure it.

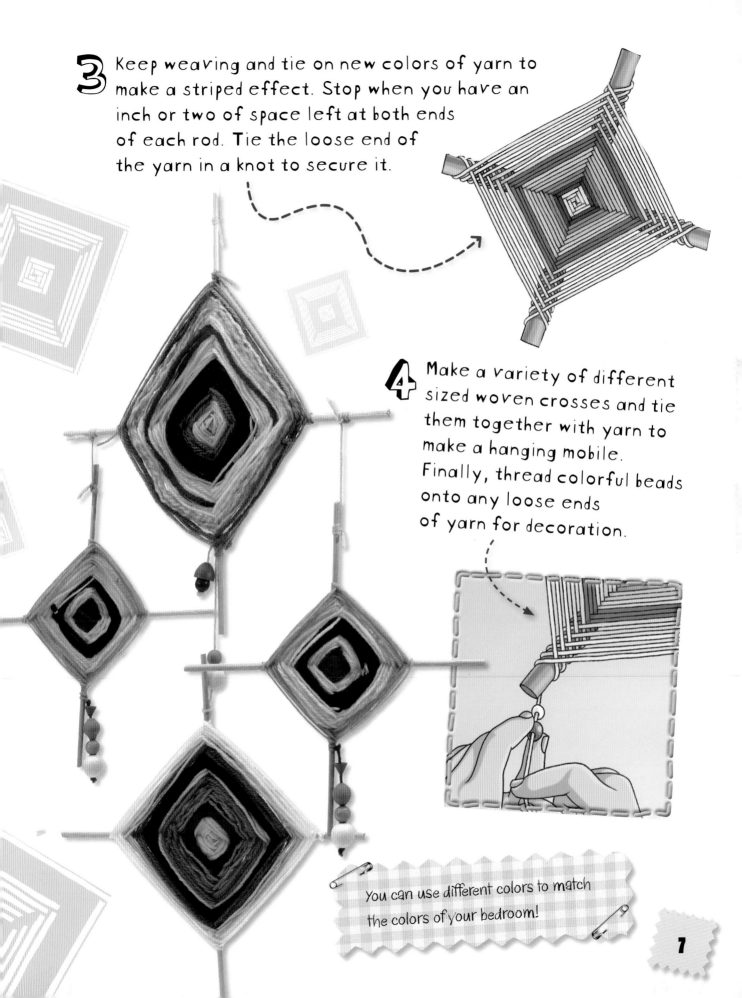

4 Make a variety of different sized woven crosses and tie them together with yarn to make a hanging mobile. Finally, thread colorful beads onto any loose ends of yarn for decoration.

You can use different colors to match the colors of your bedroom!

SPACE PILLOWCASE

Want to create a theme for your bedroom? Printing on fabric can liven up plain pillowcases.

1 Cut a piece of cardboard to fit inside your pillowcase. Insert the cardboard into the pillowcase and lie it flat.

2 Squeeze different fabric paint colors onto separate paper plates.

8

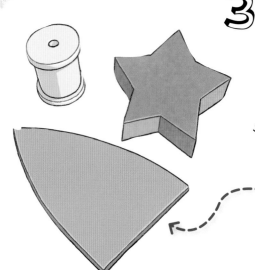

3 Use objects, such as sponges, cotton spools and cardboard shapes, to print with. Dip them into the paint and press them onto the fabric. You can cut out rocket ship or star shapes from sponge and cardboard.

4 Print your pattern all over the front of the pillowcase. Once dry, turn over and repeat on the back.

5 Once completely dry, ask an adult to place a thin cloth over the pillowcase and slowly iron over it on a cool setting. This will seal the paint and stop it from cracking or washing off.

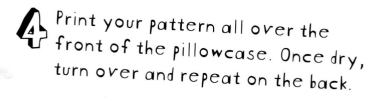

Get creative and use any colors and printing objects you like. How about a nature pattern?

POCKET ORGANIZER

Keep your bedroom tidy and stylish at the same time with this fun organizer.

YOU WILL NEED:

- Scissors
- An old piece of clothing that has pockets
- Felt in assorted colors
- Pins
- Needle
- Embroidery thread
- Fabric glue
- Sequins and goggly eyes
- Long length of ribbon
- Wooden dowel rod

1 Cut a large rectangle from an old piece of clothing, including the pockets.

2 Cut out decorative felt shapes and pin these in place on the fabric. Stick on goggly eyes if you have made any animal shapes.

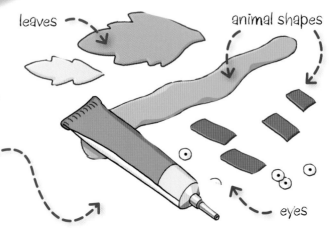

leaves

animal shapes

eyes

10

3 Stitch on the shapes using a running stitch. You can also glue or stitch on sequins to decorate your shapes.

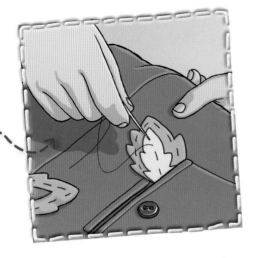

4 Using a running stitch, sew a length of ribbon around the edge of the organizer to hide the rough edges and create a border.

5 Stitch two loops of ribbon to the top of the organizer and slip a wooden dowel rod through the loops so it can be hung.

Create felt shapes that show your favorite theme. The more colorful, the better!

HAIR TIE BIRD

You can create this cute, colorful bird for a show stopping hair accessory.

YOU WILL NEED:

- Scissors
- Felt in assorted colors
- Pins
- Needle
- Embroidery thread
- Toy stuffing
- Fabric glue
- Feathers
- Goggly eyes
- Hair tie

1 Cut out two equal-sized pieces of felt for the main body shape of your bird. Pin these two pieces together.

body pieces

2 Using a needle and thread, stitch around the outside of the body in either a blanket or running stitch, leaving a space of about 1/2 inch open.

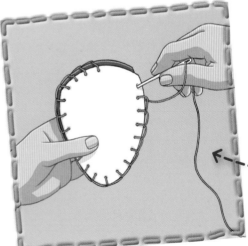

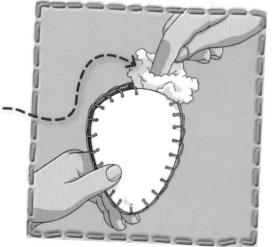

3 Through this space, fill the body with toy stuffing, then stitch up the hole.

12

4 Cut out felt ovals for the face, a folded diamond for the beak and triangles for the feathers and ears. Glue or stitch these onto the body.

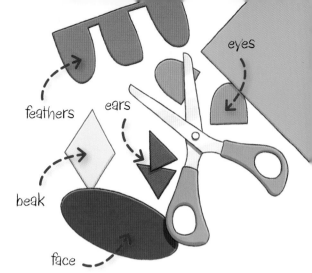

feathers

beak

ears

eyes

face

5 Attach feathers for wings and a pair of goggly eyes to make your bird come to life! Finally, stitch a hair tie to the back of the bird's body.

Make a pencil tie, using different felt shapes and colors to create any animal you want!

eyes

GET WELL CARD

This cute, colorful card will really brighten someone's day.

YOU WILL NEED:
- Nine 2 x 2 in. felt squares in assorted colors
- Needle
- Embroidery thread
- Scissors
- Felt in assorted colors
- Fabric glue
- Embroidery needle
- Lengths of yarn
- Letter-sized cardstock, folded in half

1 Lay three of the felt squares side by side and sew them together one by one, using a running stitch. Do this by holding two squares together and stitching along the very edge of one side. Repeat with the third

2 Repeat with the other squares to make three rows. Sew the rows together in the same way. Flip the quilt over so the stitching is on the back. Add a running stitch around the edge for decoration.

14

3 Make a small pillowcase by cutting out a rectangle of white felt and decorating around the edge in a running stitch.

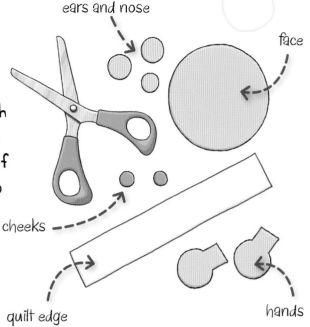

ears and nose

face

cheeks

quilt edge

hands

4 Cut out felt shapes for the face and hands. Stitch eyes and a mouth onto the face circle and glue this onto the pillowcase. Cut a strip of white felt to make a quilt edge to position the hands onto.

5 Using an embroidery needle, sew yarn around the head to make hair. Glue all the felt pieces onto a rectangle of backing felt and glue onto a folded piece of letter-sized cardstock

Who wouldn't feel better after receiving a beautiful card like this?

DINO DOORSTOP

This colorful fabric dinosaur will make the perfect little guard for your bedroom door.

YOU WILL NEED:

- Fabric chalk
- Ruler
- Different patterned fabrics
- Felt in assorted colors
- Scissors
- Needle
- Embroidery thread
- Dried beans
- Toy stuffing
- Green foam sheet
- Fabric glue
- Goggly eyes

1 With tailors' chalk, draw four equal-sided triangles on the patterned fabrics and felt. Make sure each side of each triangle is 6 inches (15 cm) long. Cut out the triangles.

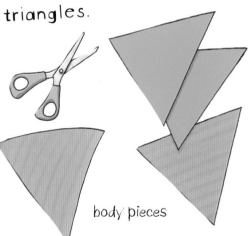

body pieces

2 With the patterned sides facing inward, use a running stitch to sew the triangles together at the sides to make a pyramid shape. Leave the final side open and turn the pyramid inside out.

3 Through the open side, fill the pyramid with dried beans. (You can use a paper cone to do this.) Sew up the open side with a blanket stitch.

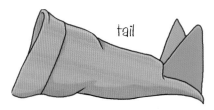

tail

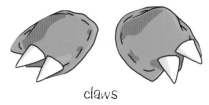

claws

4 Make a stuffed felt snout, two hands and a tail using felt shapes sewn together with a running stitch and stuffed with toy stuffing. Stitch these pieces onto the pyramid body.

5 Cut out features, such as spikes, teeth, claws, eyebrows and spots, from felt and a sheet of foam. Glue these onto the body, then stick on a pair of goggly eyes to bring your dinosaur to life!

Make a cuddly dinosaur instead by replacing the dried beans with toy stuffing.

TWISTY SOCK SNAKE

This twisty snake is cute, colorful and super-easy to make.

1 Fill a sock with toy stuffing and insert a pipe cleaner through the middle, so it is contained inside.

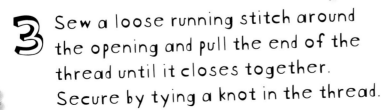

2 Tie about six rubber bands at 2 inch intervals along the sock to create the round sections of the snake's body.

3 Sew a loose running stitch around the opening and pull the end of the thread until it closes together. Secure by tying a knot in the thread.

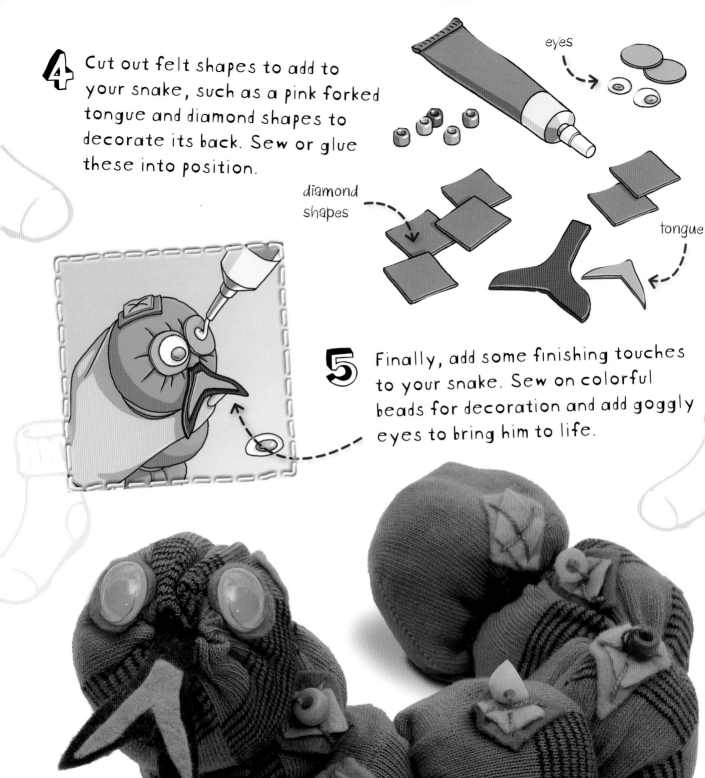

4 Cut out felt shapes to add to your snake, such as a pink forked tongue and diamond shapes to decorate its back. Sew or glue these into position.

eyes

diamond shapes

tongue

5 Finally, add some finishing touches to your snake. Sew on colorful beads for decoration and add goggly eyes to bring him to life.

A patterned sock will make your snake even more interesting.

PATCHWORK PICTURE

Pictures don't have to be painted. You can create a 3D picture using fabrics instead.

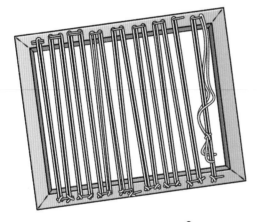

1 Wrap string around your frame, leaving 1/2 inch (1.5 cm) spaces between the lengths. Staple the threads to the back of the frame and cut off the lengths at the front.

2 Cut out about five hill shapes from paper and use these as templates to cut out hills from the patterned fabrics and felt. Make sure the hills will fit in the lower half of your frame.

3 Sew the fabric hills onto a 5 x 7 inch rectangle of green felt, using a running stitch. Leave a space in each to insert a small amount of toy stuffing before sewing them closed. Trim the top of the backing felt into a curved hill shape.

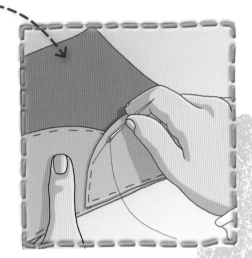

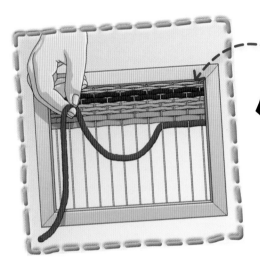

4 To make the sky, weave the ribbon and wool through the lengths of string on the frame until half the frame is filled.

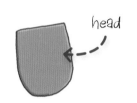
head

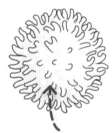
pom pom body

5 For the sheep, glue two pom poms to the hills. Cut out black felt heads and glue them into position. Finally, staple your hill landscape, facedown, to the back of your frame.

Why not try making a picture of the scene outside your window?

BURLAP POT WRAP

Work on your embroidery skills and brighten up a dull flower pot with this pretty wrap.

1 Gather the burlap fabric around the flower pot and tie it up at the top with a ribbon tied into a bow.

2 Using the fabric chalk, draw a tree design on one side of the burlap fabric. At the ends of the tree branches, draw circular shapes.

3 Begin your embroidery by using a back stitch to outline the tree trunk. Embroider the circles using colorful thread and a variety of stitches, such as chain stitch and satin stitch.

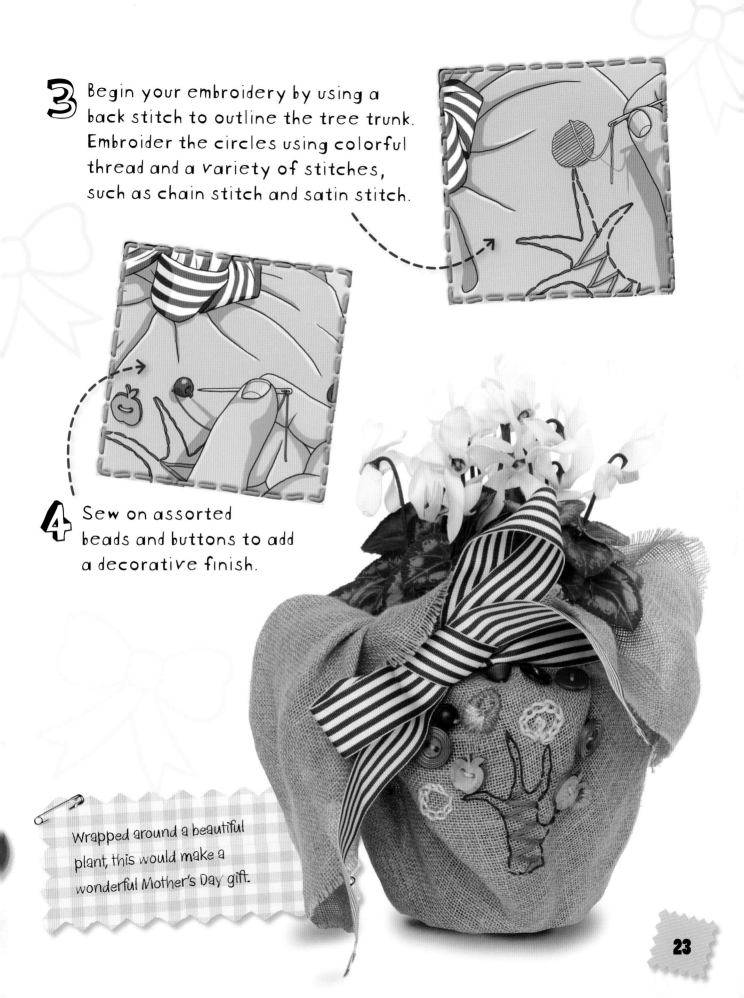

4 Sew on assorted beads and buttons to add a decorative finish.

Wrapped around a beautiful plant, this would make a wonderful Mother's Day gift.

BOUNCY BIRD

Hang this feathered friend next to your window in your room.

1 Wrap two rubber bands around a styrofoam ball so they cross over each other. Using yarn threaded onto an embroidery needle, thread the yarn over and around the rubber bands. (See page 6 for a similar method.)

2 Keep weaving until the ball is covered, changing yarn colors to make a striped effect. Tie a knot in your last thread and cut off the excess. You could leave some wool threads loose to attach beads for decoration.

3 Make a pair of wings by cutting out four identical wing shapes from felt. Sew the pairs together with a running stitch. Leave a space to insert a small amount of toy stuffing, then sew closed.

4 To make a tail, glue feathers onto the back of your bird. Glue the stiff quills under a section of woven wool. Glue or sew the wings onto the sides of the body.

5 Glue on on a folded diamond felt beak and add goggly eyes. Stitch a length of elastic thread to the ridge at the top so you can hang your bird.

Make your bird in colors that match your bedroom!

DOG PUPPET

This soft puppet is just as cute and cuddly as a real dog-but not as much work!

1 Fill a sock with toy stuffing and insert a pipe cleaner through the middle, so it is contained inside. Tie 3 rubber bands at regular spaces to create round body sections.

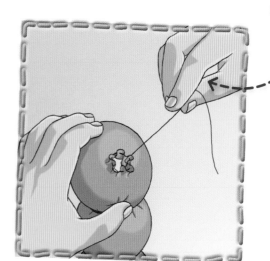

2 Sew a loose running stitch around the opening and pull the end of the thread until the opening gathers together. Tie a knot in the thread to secure.

3 Sew a running stitch all the way down the back of the sock body.

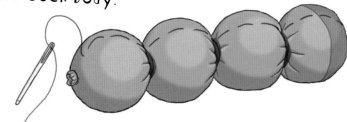

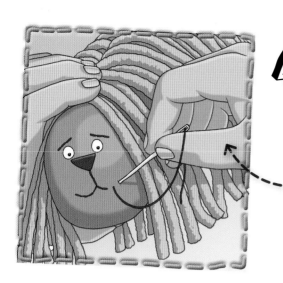

4 To make the dog's fur, thread each length of yarn through the running stitches along the back, using a large embroidery needle. Embroider a nose, mouth and eyebrows onto the face. Stick on goggly eyes.

5 Cut out two felt ears and sew these onto the head. Sew the bell onto a length of ribbon and tie around the dog's neck. Finally, make a small hole in the underside of the head, and push one dowel rod into the hole. Repeat at the other end of the body.

Make a family of dogs using different colored socks and wool.

MATERIALS

yarn

embroidery thread

Embroidery Thread
This is a type of yarn used especially for embroidery. It comes in lots of different colors.

Needles and pins
Needles are pointed metal tools to sew with. They have a hole at the top called an "eye" to thread yarn through. Pins are very similar to needles but don't have an eye at the top. They are used to hold fabric in place before sewing. Always ask an adult to help you with needles and pins. They can be very sharp.

pins

needle

Yarn
Yarn is like a very thick thread that comes in many different colors and thicknesses. It is usually used for knitting, but can be used for weaving and even embroidery.

Toy Stuffing
This is soft, white material, similar to cotton-balls. It is great for padding out your creations, to help them look more 3D. It also makes toys soft and cuddly!

toy stuffing

Fabric Paint
Fabric paint is best for painting onto fabric, as it will not wash off or bleed into the material. It will need fixing with a hot iron before washing, but always make sure an adult does this for you. Make sure whatever you are painting onto has been washed first.

fabric paint

Dowel Rods

Dowel rods are solid, lightweight sticks used for adding support to your creations. They are usually made of wood or plastic. They are easy to cut to size, but always ask an adult to do this for you.

dowel rods

Fabric Chalk

Fabric, or tailors', chalk is a very hard type of chalk that is used to make marks on fabric. It is useful to draw out shapes that you need to cut out. The marks can be washed off.

fabric chalk

Felt

This is a type of cloth that is usually soft and comes in lots of different colors. It is strong and will not fray when cut.

felt

Foam Sheets

These are thick sheets of a lightweight but tough, bendy material. You can cut them into shapes, glue them and bend them without them tearing.

foam sheet

Fabric

Fabric is any type of cloth. You can use old clothes to make your creations from, but always ask an adult before cutting anything up!

fabrics

Glue

The types of glue you'll need most when doing creative projects are white glue and fabric glue. White glue is good for sticking down paper, card, wood and almost anything. Fabric glue is better to stick fabrics, as it can be washed without coming unstuck.

glue

29

TECHNIQUES

MAKE A POM POM

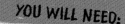

YOU WILL NEED:
- Scissors
- Cardstock
- Yarn

1 Cut two identical donut rings from cardstock and place them together.

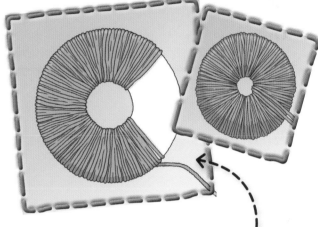

2 Wrap the wool around the rings, going through the hole and around the outer edge. Keep wrapping until the hole in the middle is very tight.

3 Cut through the yarn around the edge of the ring, a layer at a time, until you meet the cardstock rings underneath.

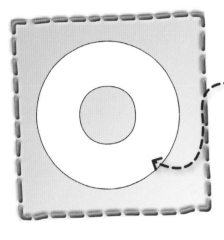

4 Pass a length of yarn in between the two cardstock rings. Tie it tightly around all the wool at the center. Now remove the cardstock rings and reveal your pom pom!

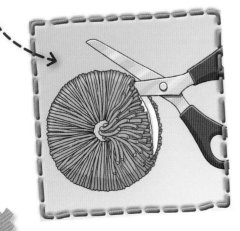

STITCHING AND WEAVING

Running stitch
Sew up and down through the fabric, making sure the stitches on both sides are kept the same size.

Blanket stitch
Push the needle through from back to front. At the front, level with your first stitch, push the needle through the fabric but come up again by going through the loop you have created with the thread.

Back stitch
Make a running stitch, then come up through the fabric a stitch ahead and stitch backwards to meet your first running stitch. Repeat in a neat line.

Weaving
Lengths of material are passed through a set of taut, spaced-out threads, in an alternate "over, under, over, under" pattern. This is repeated with many lengths so that they make an interlacing lattice. You can also weave "over and around" dowel rods in a cross shape (see woven mobile on page 6).

Chain stitch
Come up through the fabric and make a little loop, held in place with your thumb. Go back down through the fabric at the top and inside the loop. Come back up and forward a stitch length. Before pulling the needle all the way out, wrap the free thread under the needle and pull out to create your second loop.

Satin stitch
Mark out the shape you want and sew straight stitches closely together across the shape, taking care to keep the edges even.

INDEX